Giant Sequoia Trees

by Ginger Wadsworth
photographs by Frank Staub

Lerner Publications Company • Minneapolis, Minnesota

To John and Marge Hawksworth,
guardians of Nelder Grove, California
                                —GW

To Ralph
   —FS

The author wishes to thank the following people for their help:
Malinee Crapsey, Nate Stephenson, and Bill Tweed, Sequoia
National Park; Bill Evarts, author and photographer; John
Evarts, Cachuma Press; Wendy Harrison, Calaveras Big Trees;
John and Marge Hawksworth, U.S. Forest Service, Nelder Grove;
and Marjorie Popper, author and botanist.

Thanks to our series consultant, Sharyn Fenwick, elementary
science/math specialist. Mrs. Fenwick was the winner of the
National Science Teachers Association 1991 Distinguished
Teaching Award. She also was the recipient of the Presidential
Award for Excellence in Math and Science Teaching, representing
the state of Minnesota at the elementary level in 1992.

Early Bird Nature Books were conceptualized
by Ruth Berman and designed by Steve Foley.
Series editor is Joelle Goldman.

Website address: www.lernerbooks.com

Library of Congress Cataloging-in-Publication Data

Wadsworth, Ginger.
    Giant sequoia trees / by Ginger Wadsworth ; photographs by
  Frank Staub.
      p. cm—(Early bird nature books)
    Includes index.
    ISBN 0-82Z5-3001-5
    1. Giant sequoia—Juvenile literature. [1. Giant sequoia.]
  I. Staub, Frank J. II. Title. III. Series.
  QK494.5.T3W33 1995
  585'.2—dc20   94-32733

Manufactured in the United States of America
2 3 4 5 6 7 – SP – 03 02 01 00 99 98

Contents

The giant sequoia (sih-KWOY-uh) tree grows naturally only in parts of California. The red areas show exactly where sequoias live.

CANADA

N

UNITED STATES

MEXICO

Be a Word Detective

Can you find these words as you read about the sequoia tree's life? Be a detective and try to figure out what they mean. You can turn to the glossary on page 47 for help.

carbon dioxide	groves	pollination
chlorophyll	heartwood	sapwood
conifers	oxygen	seedlings
crown	photosynthesis	snag-top
germinate	pollen	understory

Chapter 1

*The scientific name of
the sequoia tree is
Sequoiadendron
giganteum. Do you
think dinosaurs ever
saw sequoia trees?*

The Largest
Living Tree

About 180 million years ago, the earth
was much warmer than it is today. Dinosaurs
roamed the forests then. The first sequoia

(sih-KWOY-uh) trees began to grow. Around 25 million years ago, sequoias were growing all across North America and Europe. But during the last million years, the earth has cooled. The sequoias began to die.

Millions of years ago, sequoia trees grew all across North America and Europe.

Today, sequoia trees grow naturally only in California. They grow on the western side of the Sierra Nevada mountains. Living with other trees and plants, sequoias are found in groups called groves. Only 75 groves of sequoias still exist.

These are the Sierra Nevada foothills in California.

About 75 groves of sequoia trees grow in an area that is only 260 miles long and 15 miles wide.

Sequoias are the largest living trees in the world. That's why they are also called giant sequoias. Sequoias can grow to be about 250 feet tall. That's the same size as a 25-story building. Their trunks can be over 30 feet wide.

The giant sequoia trees in Mariposa Grove make this museum seem like a dollhouse.

These coast redwood trees are related to sequoias. The tallest tree in the world is a coast redwood.

That's wide enough to block up to three lanes of a highway. Some sequoias weigh 10 times more than the largest animal. The largest animal is the female blue whale. Sequoias are among the oldest living things on earth. They can live for over 2,000 years.

Chapter 2

Sometimes, the leaves of a sequoia tree are called needles. Do you think leaves need water to stay green and healthy?

Parts of a Tree

All trees have three major parts. From bottom to top, each tree has roots, a trunk and branches, and leaves. The parts all work together to keep the tree alive.

Roots take water from the soil. They grow underground. But a sequoia's roots do not grow very deep. They can get water even if it rains only a little bit. Adult sequoias need thousands of gallons of water each day. We only need about half a gallon of water a day. Half a gallon of water fills eight cups. Sequoias get most of their water from melted snow that has soaked into the ground. The water travels up the tree's trunk to the leaves.

Roots grow underground. Some of the roots of this sequoia tree were pulled out of the ground when it fell and died.

Trunks and branches have many layers. The outer layer is called the bark. The sequoia's bark can be 2 feet thick. It protects the tree. On hot summer days, bark keeps the tree cool. During the winter, bark works like a blanket. It protects the tree from cold, wind, and snow.

Sequoia bark feels soft and stringy. You can see how thick the bark is on this small sequoia stump.

This sequoia crashed to the ground and broke. Now you can see the yellowish sapwood and pinkish heartwood.

Wood is the next layer. All trees have two kinds of wood. The sapwood is closest to the bark. Water travels from the roots through the sapwood to the leaves. Heartwood is in the center of the trunk. It helps keep the tree strong and standing tall.

Leaves help make food for the tree.

The leaves on the sequoia branches are
short and prickly. They overlap one another like
a braided rope. The top of the tree, where all
the leaves are, is called the crown.

All green plants and trees, including sequoias, need food to live. And all green plants make their own food. Plants are green because they have chlorophyll (KLOR-uh-fihl). Chlorophyll turns sunlight into energy. Leaves use this energy to make food.

Sunlight helps trees make their own food.

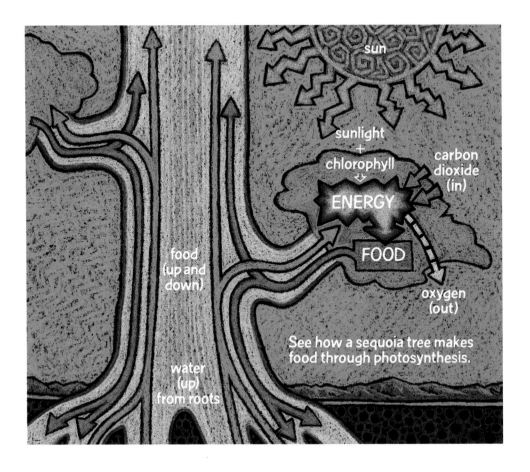

labels within the image:
sun
sunlight
+
chlorophyll
carbon dioxide (in)
ENERGY
FOOD
oxygen (out)
food (up and down)
water (up) from roots
See how a sequoia tree makes food through photosynthesis.

The way plants make food is called photosynthesis (foh-toh-SIHN-thuh-sihs). Water is pulled up from the roots, through the sapwood, into the crown of the tree. At the same time, the leaves take in a gas called carbon dioxide (dy-AHK-side) from the air. Chlorophyll uses energy from sunlight to change water and

We breathe out carbon dioxide, which plants need to make food. Plants make oxygen, which we need to breathe.

carbon dioxide into food. The food travels from the leaves to the branches, trunk, and roots.

During photosynthesis, trees make oxygen (AHKS-uh-jihn). Oxygen is a gas that is part of the air we breathe. Oxygen escapes through the leaves and joins the air. So trees help make the air we breathe.

Chapter 3

A sequoia tree starts growing cones when it is about 10 years old. How many cones do you think adult sequoias grow every year?

From Seed to Tree

Sequoias are conifers (KAHN-uh-fuhrz). Fir, spruce, and pine trees are conifers too. Most conifers are evergreens. Conifers are plants that have cones. There are male cones and female cones. Adult sequoias make about 2,000 new cones each year.

Female cones are the part of a conifer that holds the seeds. Sequoia cones are the size and shape of chickens' eggs. These cones protect the seeds. Up to 300 seeds fit inside each sequoia cone.

Sequoia seeds are the size of a flake of oatmeal. It takes 91,000 seeds to weigh 1 pound.

During the winter, a yellow powder called pollen bursts out of male cones. The pollen drifts in the wind. Some of the pollen reaches the female cones. This is called pollination (pahl-uh-NAY-shun). Seeds start to grow inside the female cones. A few years go by before the seeds are ready to grow into sequoia trees.

Seeds have already dropped out of the brown cones. The green cone still contains its seeds.

The golden-mantled ground squirrel is one of the animals who eat sequoia cones.

Seeds drop out of the cones in different ways. Some animals like Douglas squirrels eat sequoia cones, dropping the seeds to the ground. Sometimes, strong winds rip cones off branches. Sequoias also need forest fires to get seeds out of their cones.

The black marks on this sequoia's trunk are burn scars from fires.

Forest fires are important to sequoias. Nearly every summer, thunderstorms blow across the Sierra Nevada. Lightning often starts ground fires. Cones grow on the sequoia's crown. They are usually too high to burn during a forest fire. But they do become dry from the fire's heat.

After the fire, the scales on the cone open. The seeds flutter out of the cones onto the ground. A thin layer of ash from the fire covers the seeds. The ash helps the seeds grow.

These young white firs are growing well because of a fire that burned a year ago.

Fires burn the forest understory. The understory is the smaller trees and plants that live in the shade of tall trees. After the understory dies, the sequoia seeds can grow better. They do not have to share the water and good soil with the other plants. More sunlight reaches the forest

The understory is full and green beneath the sequoias' crowns.

Young sequoias grow in an area where there is no understory.

floor. Many scientists believe experts should start fires from time to time to burn the understory. Then the new sequoia seeds would have a better chance to grow.

Only a few sequoia seedlings grow into trees. Some are eaten by animals. Others don't get enough sunlight or water during their first few years.

In the spring, the seeds are ready to germinate (JUR-muh-nayt), or grow. The tiny trees, called seedlings, push out of the soil. By late summer or fall, the seedlings are 1 to 2 inches tall. The new leaves are green on the top side and reddish on the bottom side. At first, the trunks are brown. As the sequoias grow, hundreds of roots spread out just a few feet below the soil.

A sequoia seedling grows in the sunlight.

For the first 250 years, sequoias look like upside-down ice-cream cones. Then their trunks begin to turn red. When they are about 500 to 700 years old, sequoias reach their full height. The crowns look rounded. Most of the low branches break off and fall to the ground. The trunks are bare for 100 to 150 feet, or more.

These young sequoias look like upside-down ice-cream cones.

As they grow older, sequoias grow bigger branches and thicker trunks to help keep their balance.

High on the trunks, twisted branches spread out like large arms. For the rest of their lives, sequoias grow bigger branches and thicker trunks. Thick branches and trunks help trees keep their balance. So do the roots. They cling to the ground and to other roots.

Chapter 4

The bark of this sequoia tree is dotted with black burn scars. Do you think sequoia bark burns easily?

Death of a Sequoia

Most old sequoias die after they fall over in a powerful wind or snowstorm. Sometimes, fires weaken the tree and the roots. Sequoia bark doesn't burn easily though. It protects the tree from most fires. Bark helps sequoias live a long life. But some fires are so hot that a sequoia's trunk does burn. Then the tree is covered with black scars. The scars can cut off water flow from the roots to other parts of the tree. Branches die when they do not get water. Often the rest of the tree keeps growing. When part of the crown dies, the tree is called a snag-top. Many sequoias look strange because they are snag-tops.

Part of the crown has died on this snag-top.

A large sequoia crashing to the ground
shakes the earth. Part of a dead sequoia might
lie on the forest floor for hundreds of years.

A dead sequoia lies across the forest floor.

Carpenter ants have found a home in this sequoia's trunk.

Spiders, mice, birds, squirrels, and other small animals make homes in the roots and bigger branches. Woodpeckers drill for ants and other insects. Fires burn through the forest. The wood cracks and crumbles. Little by little, the tree becomes part of the soil.

A white fir seedling grows out of a dead sequoia.

Like a huge time-release pill, the tree gives
vitamins back to the earth. Nearby, other new
plants and trees, including sequoia seedlings,
start to grow in the rich soil.

Top: *Bright red snow plants grow in the rich forest soil.*

Left: *Dead sequoias are rich with food and vitamins, so plants, like this bedstraw, can grow on them.*

37

A ranger is pointing out the growth rings on a sequoia tree stump. Do you think scientists can tell the age of a tree?

The Sequoia's Future

Today, scientists are learning more about sequoias. Each year, a dark and light circle forms in the trunk as a tree grows. The dark part of the circle is called the growth ring. The dark rings are wide during wet years, when the tree grows a lot. They are narrow during dry years, when the tree grows only a little bit. Scientists can count a tree's growth rings. They study the rings to learn the age and history of each tree.

Scientists interested in the history of this old giant sequoia tree can study its growth rings.

Most sequoias are in national forests or parks. Every year, millions of visitors from around the world travel to the groves. Paved roads cover the rich soil and shallow roots. The visitors walk around and around each tree. Their feet make the ground hard. The roots have trouble soaking up water. This is killing some of the

A road cuts through Sequoia National Park, making it hard for nearby sequoia trees to get water.

The General Sherman Tree is the biggest sequoia. It is over 274 feet high, and its trunk is over 102 feet around at the ground.

GENERAL SHERMAN

sequoias. People want to see the largest, the oldest, and the most unusual-looking sequoia trees. They take pictures. They buy seeds to take home and plant.

Young sequoia trees grow in a forest of big sequoias and other trees.

Now, young sequoias are growing all over the world. Some of them are only an inch or two high. Others are taller than a two-story house. But hundreds of years from now, these sequoias could be as large as the Grizzly Giant or the General Sherman trees. And near the big trees, new sequoia seedlings will begin to grow.

Big sequoias, like the Grizzly Giant, are not the oldest sequoias. They are the sequoias that grow the fastest.

On Sharing a Book

As you know, adults greatly influence a child's attitude toward reading. When a child sees you read, or when you share a book with a child, you're sending a message that reading is important. Show the child that reading a book together is important to you. Find a comfortable, quiet place. Turn off the television and limit other distractions, such as telephone calls.

Be prepared to start slowly. Take turns reading parts of this book. Stop and talk about what you're reading. Talk about the photographs. You may find that much of the shared time is spent discussing just a few pages. This discussion time is valuable for both of you, so don't move through the book too quickly. If the child begins to lose interest, stop reading. Continue sharing the book at another time. When you do pick up the book again, be sure to revisit the parts you have already read. Most importantly, enjoy the book!

Be a Vocabulary Detective

You will find a word list on page 5. Words selected for this list are important to the understanding of the topic of this book. Encourage the child to be a word detective and search for the words as you read the book together. Talk about what the words mean and how they are used in the sentence. Do any of these words have more than one meaning? You will find these words defined in a glossary on page 47.

What about Questions?

Use questions to make sure the child understands the information in this book. Here are some suggestions:

> What did this paragraph tell us? What does this picture show? What do you think we'll learn about next? How are sequoia trees different from the trees in our yard? How are they similar? Name other plants and animals that live with sequoias. How do sequoia trees make food? How do they help other plants and animals even when they are dead? How do fires help sequoias? How do fires hurt sequoias? What is your favorite part of the book? Why?

If the child has questions, don't hesitate to respond with questions of your own, such as: What do *you* think? Why? What is it that you don't know? If the child can't remember certain facts, turn to the index.

Introducing the Index

The index is an important learning tool. It helps readers get information quickly without searching throughout the whole book. Turn to the index on page 48. Choose an entry, such as *cones,* and ask the child to use the index to find out how many new cones grow on a sequoia each year. Repeat this exercise with as many entries as you like. Ask the child to point out the differences between an index and a glossary. (The index helps readers find information quickly, while the glossary tells readers what words mean.)

All the World in Metric!

Although our monetary system is in metric units (based on multiples of 10), the United States is one of the few countries in the world that does not use the metric system of measurement. Here are some conversion activities you and the child can do using a calculator:

WHEN YOU KNOW:	MULTIPLY BY:	TO FIND:
miles	1.609	kilometers
feet	0.3048	meters
inches	2.54	centimeters
gallons	3.787	liters
tons	0.907	metric tons
pounds	0.454	kilograms

Activities

Go to a park and count the number of conifers you see. Look for cones and see how many different kinds you can find. Look at the branches. How many different kinds of leaves or needles can you find? Do you see any animals on these trees?

Make a tree book. Punch a hole in some papers. Tie a short piece of string through the hole. Have each page or couple of pages represent a particular type of tree. Glue or tape down leaves, needles, bark, and any other parts of a tree. Draw a picture of each tree. Compare the trees in your book to sequoia trees.

Spend some time watching a tree. What kinds of animals use the tree? How do they use the tree? How many animals live on the tree? Now write a story about some of these animals and their activities in the tree.

Glossary

carbon dioxide (dy-AHK-side)—a gas in the air that is taken in by plants and used to make food

chlorophyll (KLOR-uh-fihl)—the green color in a plant's leaves or stem that makes photosynthesis possible

conifers (KAHN-uh-fuhrz)—trees or shrubs with cones. Most conifers are evergreen.

crown—the branches and leaves of a tree

germinate (JUR-muh-nayt)—to start growing

groves—groups of trees growing together

heartwood—the hard, strong, wood of a tree that is at the center of the trunk

oxygen (AHKS-uh-jihn)—a gas that plants give off to the air and we need to breathe

photosynthesis (foh-toh-SIHN-thuh-sihs)—the way green plants use the energy from sunlight to make food out of carbon dioxide and water

pollen—yellow dust that is needed to make seeds

pollination (pahl-uh-NAY-shun)—the movement of pollen from the male part to the female part so seeds can form

sapwood—the soft wood of a tree that is closest to the bark

seedlings—young plants

snag-top—a tree that has a partly dead crown

understory—the short trees and plants that grow in the shade of tall trees

47

Index

Pages listed in **bold** type
refer to photographs.